PRAISE FOR
CYBERCRISIS

* * * * *

"**CYBERCRISIS** will wake you up from a nightmare you didn't even know you were in. Once again, William Keiper has written a book that shines a light for the rest of us."
~Steve Chandler, author of *Time Warrior*

"**CYBERCRISIS** answers the question, 'How can we harness the value of internet technology without opening the door to our real-lives?'"
~Stephen McGhee, Transformational Leadership Coach and author of *Climb to Freedom* and *Get Real*

CYBERCRISIS
IT'S PERSONAL NOW

CYBERCRISIS
IT'S PERSONAL NOW

WILLIAM KEIPER

FirstGlobal® Partners LLC
dba FirstGlobal® Publishing

Copyright © 2016 William Keiper
All rights reserved. No part of this book may be reproduced or copied
in any form without the permission of the publisher. Thank you
for your support of the author's rights.
Contact the publisher: www.firstglobalpartners.com
Contact the author: www.williamkeiper.com

Chris Nelson, editor
David Moratto, interior and cover design
Alex Cyrell, creative consultant
Selim Aksan, cover photograph (iStock by Getty Images)
Tracy Rasinski, author photo

The material provided herein is for general information and educational purposes only. Although the publisher and author use reasonable efforts to include accurate and up-to-date information herein, no warranties or representations of any kind as to accuracy, currency, or completeness are made. Because of the dynamic nature of the internet, any Web addresses or links contained in this book may have changed since publication and may no longer be valid.

This book is sold with the understanding that the publisher and author do not intend and are not engaged in rendering psychiatric or psychological, medical, legal, or other advice requiring licensure or certification. The information contained herein may not apply to all situations and may not reflect the most current situation.

Rather than use a trademark symbol with every usage of a trademarked name, such names are used only in an editorial fashion and to the benefit of the trademark owner, with no intention of infringement, confusion or ambiguity as to ownership. All marks are the property of their respective companies.

Library of Congress Control Number: 2016958606
ISBN-10: 0-9913835-0-8 and ISBN-13: 978-0-9913835-0-4
ISBN-10: 098498934X and ISBN-13: 978-0-9849893-4-8 electronic

*For inspiration and support in the creation,
execution and completion of*
CYBERCRISIS—It's Personal Now:

*Chris Nelson, Jim Manton, Stephen McGhee,
Alex Cyrell, Steve Chandler, Jeff Holtmeier,
David Moratto, Mary Aiken, Ph.D.,
and my wife, Pamala Plummer-Wright.*

CONTENTS

INTRODUCTION — THE WEB IS US, WE ARE THE WEB xi

1. YOU'VE BEEN HACKED 1
2. "I'M NOT ADDICTED ... I'M LIKE YOU" 9
3. CYBERSLACKERS: ONLINE COMPULSION GOES TO WORK 19
4. A BILLION SOCIAL NETWORK DUPES AND FAKERS 25
5. ANYTHING YOU SHARE MAY BE USED AGAINST YOU 31
6. YOUR ONLINE REPUTATION PRECEDES YOU 39
7. CYBERCRIME PAYS 45
8. THE HIDDEN WEB 51
9. YOUR WEB ACCESS ROUTINE 59
9. PERSONAL CYBERSECURITY: WHAT TO DO 63

GLOSSARY 67
WILLIAM KEIPER — AUTHOR BIO & RECOGNITION 73

INTRODUCTION
THE WEB IS US, WE ARE THE WEB

Click-by-click you are being pulled more deeply into the personalized slice of cyberspace you have created and shaped through your choices.

Each click holds the promise of enhancing your life through immediate access to unlimited online resources of every kind. Each click can expand your social interactions and increase your visibility, far and wide if you choose. Each click also has the potential for sending you into the den of a bad actor wanting to take your money, or with an even darker purpose.

The distinction that has been drawn between "real-life" and "online life," is fading to the point where it's hard to see. However, your online activities often expose you to threats, risks, and consequences in contexts that are quite different from real-life. The patterns you quickly recognize from your accumulation of real-life experiences, often don't translate well enough or fast enough to be of value in your online world.

The principal objective of *CYBERCRISIS - It's Personal Now* is to heighten your awareness of some of the factors and conditions that could, in the blink of any eye, suck you into a personal cybercrisis. It represents a warning shot for those of you predisposed to trust your fellow man in the real-world and, without thinking, carry that bias into cyberspace.

Behaviors held in check in the real-world may be readily pursued online. Some of these include voluntarily handing over deeply personal information to strangers, posting a mean, anonymous comment in an online forum, or creating a fake profile as a way of checking up on a spouse or boyfriend.

For purposes of this book, I have assumed that you use a smartphone, email, apps, messaging and social networks, but are not a technology expert. My perspective as the author comes from having been a part of computer technology and software businesses since shortly after the launch of the first Apple and IBM personal computers.

In these public and private technology and related companies, I have served as CEO, board member, and strategic advisor. Through this work, I gained experience, understanding, and perspective, about digital age developments and their personal impacts, good and bad. I have also written two previous books whose driving themes involve greater self-reliance in personal and business life. My hope is that this book will motivate you to accept a higher level of personal responsibility for your digital well-being.

This is not a technical manual about cybersecurity and the most bulletproof ways to protect yourself from Web threats. I do, however, offer some personal cybersafety tips and references in Chapters Nine and Ten. I also provide a Glossary for your reference in understanding terms that may be unfamiliar to you.

Even if you are a technology expert, comfortable with digital technology, or already consider yourself a safe navigator of cyberspace, you may discover some interesting facts and perspectives within these pages.

I chose to keep this book as brief as possible. You should be able to read it in about sixty to ninety minutes. To help speed you along your way, I elected to forego footnotes and other research citations, with a few exceptions. The numbers and other facts stated here are based on data and information I personally researched, and most of which can readily be discovered by keyword or phrase search.

The Web is us, and we as a collective are the Web. After reading *CYBERCRISIS,* my hope is that you will better understand this dynamic relationship, and appreciate the need for self-reliance in cyberspace, just as much as in the real-world.

~William Keiper
www.williamkeiper.com

The illusion is that the cyber environment is safer than real-life —and connecting with other people online somehow carries fewer risks than face-to-face contact ... [However] our instincts, which were honed for the real-world, fail us in cyberspace.
~Mary Aiken, Ph.D., *The Cyber Effect, A Pioneering Cyberpsychologist Explains How Human Behavior Changes Online*

* * * * * * *

ONE
YOU'VE BEEN HACKED

Your personal information will be hacked if it hasn't been already. When such access has been accomplished, the result is called a data breach; unfortunately, this is a term we know all too well these days. These violations are designed to disrupt the information status quo for economic, political, social and religious reasons. They also are sometimes pursued to gain an advantage in the pursuit of criminal activities or simply for hackers to prove it can be done.

Although the definition of hacking sounds impersonal "Using computers to obtain unauthorized access to data," most significant data breaches sweep up a huge number of individuals.

COLLATERAL DAMAGE

Global enterprises, mid-sized companies, governments around the world, and even the major internet infrastructure companies, face increasingly frequent disruption and the damage associated with data breaches. The impact of hacks on very large-scale information systems is costly and dangerous for the institutions that are targeted, and harmful for their shareholders.

These hacks often become very personal. The Federal Trade Commission has reported that the number one consumer complaint lodged for the past fifteen years running has been identity theft—one significant consequence when vast amounts of personal information are stolen in larger data breaches.

The Yahoo data breach, the largest ever, significantly increased the number of identities publicly exposed this year over last. The following excerpt from an article in *The New York Times* describes how such a massive and seemingly distant data breach—*reported by Yahoo two years after it happened*—can become your problem.

> SAN FRANCISCO—Yahoo announced on Thursday that the account information of at least 500 million users was stolen by hackers two years ago, in the biggest known intrusion of one company's computer network. In a statement, Yahoo said user information—including names, email addresses, telephone numbers, birth dates, encrypted passwords and, in some cases, security questions—was compromised [two years before this article appeared] … "The stolen Yahoo data is critical because it not only leads to a single system but to users' connections to their banks, social media profiles, other financial services and users' friends and family," said Alex Holden, the founder of Hold Security, which has been tracking the flow of stolen Yahoo credentials on the underground Web. "This is one of the biggest breaches of people's privacy and very far reaching."

If you want to know if your personal information was compromised in the Yahoo (or another) data breach, you can go to www.haveibeenpwned.com, a website dedicated to informing victims of data breaches. [Pwned (sounds like owned) is another word for hacked.] Once there, enter your email address, verify that you control it, and a search will be made of Pwned's hundreds of millions of records. As for known breaches, any released information in which your email address has been found, will be reported to you.

"AM I UNDER SURVEILLANCE?"

It's no wonder that Americans have a significant feeling of data insecurity. Pew Internet Research discovered low levels of confidence in the privacy and security of the personal data records maintained by many of the companies and financial institutions with which they do business.

Pew also found that "Americans have a pervasive sense that they are under surveillance when in public and very few feel they have significant control over the data that is collected about them and how it is used."

A few examples from the Pew studies:

- 93% of adults say that being in control of *who* can get information about them is important.
- 90% say that controlling *what* information is collected about them is important.
- Just 9% of adults say they are "very confident," and 29% say they are "somewhat confident," their data will stay private and secure with credit card companies.
- Just 6% of adults say they are "very confident" that government agencies can keep their records private and secure, while another 25% say they are "somewhat confident."

Despite these sentiments, the door to our personal data largely remains open, often through our own negligence. We don't choose options readily available to us that could keep it at least partially closed. (See Chapters Nine and Ten.)

At the level of our own smartphones, tablets, and PCs, we open ourselves to data breaches through the most pervasive of today's communication methods: email and messaging. Symantec produces software for security, storage, and backup, and offers well-researched findings on the subjects. They reported the following on the topic of email:

- For cybercriminals who want to reach the largest number of people electronically, email is still the favored way to do it. It continues to dominate digital communications for both business and consumer use.
- Total worldwide email traffic, including both business and consumer emails, is estimated to grow to over 257 billion emails per *day* by the end of 2020. About half of all inbound email traffic last year was considered spam.

- Email is widely used as the delivery mechanism for spam, phishing, and malware, and all have potentially significant harmful consequences.
- Malware distributed in emails requires social engineering [making the desired action seem familiar and comfortable for the user] to convince its recipient to open the attachment or to click on a link.

Even given their ongoing success using email as a primary delivery vehicle, spammers have now pervasively infiltrated social networking and instant messaging, two of the most-used mobile applications.

DATA FINGERPRINT

McAfee.com, now a part of Intel Security, a provider of security solutions and services, has said that "Data is the 'oil,'" of the digital economy. The oil, specifically, is your personal information when exploited on three fronts. First, your continuous enrollment and participation in social communities so as to drive advertising and other revenues for the platform owners. Second, your personal information when unlocked and made available for purchase by third-parties. And third, the ransoming of your identity or other data crucial for conducting your life.

The core value element in these instances is your personally identifiable information (abbreviated as "PII"). The National Institute of Standards and Technology (NIST) defines PII as:

> "Any information about an individual maintained by an agency, including (1) any information that can be used to distinguish or trace an individual's identity, such as name, social security number, date and place of birth, mother's maiden name, or biometric records; and (2) any other information that is linked or linkable to an individual, such as medical, educational, financial, and employment information."

I prefer to call this your "data fingerprint" because it is unique, like a fingerprint. This term has been popularized by Terbium Labs, a company that will monitor the Hidden Web (see Chapter Eight) for online mentions of the personal information embodied in your data fingerprint.

The information described in the Yahoo data breach referenced above represents the personal data you regularly offer in an enrollment process with a service provider. At such time, you voluntarily —and probably without much thought—provide a good portion of your complete data fingerprint. Typically, you authorize this by agreeing to the site's terms and conditions: long and complex verbiage you don't read. This information helps those companies monetize your membership through the sale of upgrades and other services, and by selling advertising.

PUBLIC EXPOSURE

The consequences of a personal data breach can include the pain and possible embarrassment caused by the exposure of information expected to remain private. Last year, this became sensationally clear with the public release of the identities of users of the Ashley Madison site. Ashley Madison is an adult dating site that once advertised, "Life is Short, Have an Affair!" Because the purpose of the site was to make it easier for spouses to cheat, people enrolled with the expectation that their personal information would stay private: names, credit card data, physical addresses and sexual preferences.

A group calling itself "The Impact Team" hacked the Ashley Madison site and demanded that it be taken down in protest of certain of the company's business practices, and its encouragement of adultery. With Ashley Madison's ongoing refusal to close the site, the hacked data—encompassing an estimated 32,000,000 user accounts —was released. Individual account details were initially posted to the Dark Web. They were later found to include the names, passwords, addresses, phone numbers and credit card transactions of the site's millions of users.

Very shortly after that, it became a simple matter to enter your spouse's email as an online query on Have I Been Pwned, and other sites, and instantly learn if his or her email address was part of the Ashley Madison data release. You can imagine the conversations that many couples must have had shortly after the news broke of the hack, and then the public release of the records. Although it was a huge breach at the time—just last year—ironically, it no longer makes the Top 10 largest data breaches.

This year a similar organization, known as AdultFriendFinder.com, suffered an even more far-reaching hack. It involved over 412 million user accounts. Over 99% of the user passwords were cracked. Bigger and more popular than Ashley Madison, the hack included email addresses and passwords collected over twenty years. Much like Ashley Madison, however, the details of users who believed their accounts had long ago been deleted, were stolen—in this case for the *second* time in a year.

YOU WILL BE HACKED

Information security is far from bulletproof, and even the best companies, financial institutions, and governments are not able to keep up with technical assaults by hackers. We have witnessed large-scale hacks of major companies leading to the exposure of a total approaching a billion personal identities—*just in the past year*. Corporate record and website data breaches, the release of government files, and intrusions on your own devices, are the vehicles for public exposure of the private information that is your identity.

The more complete the personal information associated with your name, the more credible your data fingerprint, and the easier it is to successfully commit identity theft. A full set of personal information (called "fullz") means a higher potential price should it be made available for sale. (See Chapter 8, The Hidden Web.)

The days when you could expect, and have reasonable confidence, that information about you would remain private, are over. You must proceed on the assumption that who and what you are in private, will one day be examined in the light of day.

There is now and always will be an onslaught of email- and messaging-borne intrusions into your smartphone, apps, and personal data, by unknown assailants. If the past few years are any guide, large data breaches will result in the release of hundreds of millions of full or partial data fingerprints each year.

The Web is important, even essential, to us humans. But it is a highly flawed environment when it comes to ease of exploitation by bad actors. Remember the fighter's admonition: "Protect yourself at all times."

TWO
"I'M NOT ADDICTED; I'M LIKE YOU..."

Magicians start by looking for blind spots, edges, vulnerabilities, and limits of people's perception ... Once you know how to push people's buttons, you can play them like a piano.
~Tristan Harris, former Design Ethicist
and Product Philosopher at Google

It is not a phone.

It's a highly advanced technological device with immense utility. A full-fledged computing device that is smaller than a wallet. But we still call it a phone. We add "smart" as a modifier as if that somehow will encompass the vast differences between it and what was once a device principally used for voice communication. Within two years, over 85% of the population is expected to access the internet from their smartphones. Most users in the United States already do.

For most of us, it is the pulse of our lives.

Neither "internet" nor "social network" addiction is yet officially recognized by the psychiatric community. However, it is no secret that our connection with the devices that enable access to the Web, contains an element of urgency and compulsion, sometimes to an extreme. As you observe those around you, it is evident that whatever is driving their almost non-stop connection with the online world can turn mere internet access into an obsession.

Let's take a closer look at some of our typical interactions:

- The average smartphone user checks their device over 200 times per day, more than 1,500 times per week.
- Seven in ten young smartphone owners check their devices more often, including 22% who admit to checking it every few minutes.

- Most American smartphone users keep their phones near them all day, and about 75% of Americans with or near them while sleeping. For a 3% minority, the phone stays in their hands while sleeping.
- About half of smartphone owners say it is something "... they couldn't live without."

NORMAL, OR NOT ABNORMAL?

A survey of 1,300 parents and children by Common Sense Media, found that 59% of parents believe their teens are addicted to mobile devices. Fifty percent of those teenagers agree with their parents (on this single point anyway). Twenty-eight percent of teens feel their parents may suffer the same addiction.

The study also concluded that 48% of parents and 72% of teens believe they must answer emails and texts *immediately*—with no waiting. Have you gotten a little miffed at this kind of interruption when you were in the middle of a conversation (or at dinner) with a message recipient?

With over six billion iPhones and other smartphones in use, persistent usage is the accepted norm. Could it be that these devices are at the core of a nationwide (if not global) personal addiction?

I suspect that serious consideration will be made for the inclusion of "Internet addiction" as a disorder recognized by the Diagnostic and Statistical Manual for Mental Disorders (DSM). As interest intensifies in the "psychopathological effects" of the use of smartphones and similar devices, it is a compelling candidate for such a label.

Allen Frances, a Professor Emeritus at Duke University (and chairman of the DSM-IV task force), wrote, "Most of us spend a good part of our days in front of a screen, both professionally and recreationally. For many, the first and last act of the day is on a screen, with multiple interactions through the day and in the middle of the night ... Are we all addicted? ... If taken beyond its narrowest usage, 'behavioral addiction' would expand the definition of mental disorder to its breaking point and would threaten to *erase the concept of normality*." (Emphasis added.)

In other words, almost all of us are at least somewhat compulsive users of smartphones. But, because there are so many of us in the category, it is considered normal behavior. Or, at least not abnormal. No matter the pervasiveness of usage, there is a point that when passed, indicates potential addiction.

How can you tell if you might be addicted or at least obsessed? Dr. Kimberly S. Young, the founder of the Center for Internet Addiction, created the IADQ—Internet Addiction Diagnostic Questionnaire—to evaluate possible internet addiction. The questions resemble those used to assess the likelihood of alcohol or drug addiction.

Below are some of the queries. According to Dr. Young, answering positively to five or more of them may be indicative of an online addiction. I have supplemented her questions with some of my own (in italics) for your further consideration.

- Are you preoccupied with using the internet? Do you think about your previous or future online activity? *Do you find your online world more compelling than your real-world? Do you plan your day for breaks to catch up with what you may have missed in your cyberworld?*
- Do you have the need to be online longer to be satisfied? *Do you experience loneliness or unhappiness when you are offline? Are you sleeping less because of your internet use?*
- Have you made repeated but unsuccessful attempts to cut back, stop or control your internet use? *Although you try, is being online something that you cannot resist for more than a short period? Do you have feelings of guilt when you are online, believing it is inappropriate?*
- Do you become moody, restless, irritable or depressed when you stop or decrease your internet use? *Do you fight with those around you about their insistence on some face-to-face attention? Do you resent having to go to dinner or social gatherings with your family and others?*
- Is your time spent online longer than what you originally planned? *Does time pass without your being aware of how long it has been since you logged on? Do you leave important*

- tasks undone? *Have you missed appointments that shouldn't have been missed?*
- Did your online use negatively affect a significant relationship, education, career or job? *Would you rather be enjoying your online relationships than tending to those you are a part of in the real-world?*
- Do you conceal the extent of your internet usage from your therapist, family or others? *Do you make up stories about being someplace other than online? Do you escape to private areas to not be noticed when online? Do you ever feel ashamed about your internet usage?*
- Does the internet serve as an escape from problems or relief from a bad mood? *Instead of choosing real-world activities (a walk or a visit with a friend) as a way of changing the scene and shifting your state of mind, do you default by going or staying online?*

Even if *you* do not have any of the indicators of online addiction, I suggest you go back through these questions and answer them with your children, other members of your family, social circle and co-workers in mind. If you feel that you or someone close to you may have an internet or other addiction, please seek out a licensed professional for a consultation.

All of us have a level of attachment to smartphones as devices of high utility. They enable us to be more productive and connected in many areas of our personal and professional lives. Given the pervasiveness of internet use today for work, online banking, entertainment, education and more, determining what degree of usage is too much, is highly dependent upon personality and circumstances.

A POCKET SLOT

Because gambling is an addiction already recognized by the psychiatry community, let's compare electronic casino games with smartphones.

Casinos and the games within them have been designed to keep your attention for as long as possible. Writing for *New Republic* magazine, Alice Robb interviewed Natasha Schüll, the author of *Addiction by Design: Machine Gambling in Las Vegas*. Ms. Schüll said:

> The cultural history of gambling in this country follows alongside technological advances—not only because technology makes these new kinds of machines possible, but because we've become comfortable interacting with and even trusting computers and machines ... I can't tell you how often I've been approached by Silicon Valley types who say things like, "Wow, the gambling industry really seems to have a handle on this attention retention problem that we're all facing. Will you come tell our designers how to do a better job?"

Should we be surprised?

Could it be that smartphones have been designed with the objective of getting us hooked to one degree or another? This could explain why an average smartphone user, as noted above, checks it about 1,500 times per week.

Consider the similarities between an electronic video poker or slot machine and a smartphone. Both have been engineered to be slick, attractive, comfortable and compelling. Both have vibrant, high-resolution video screens, digital audio, streaming video, soundtracks, flashing lights, vibrations, ringing and other sounds.

In both cases, constant attention to the device is reinforced by the delivery of intermittent variable rewards. These are handed out or enforced inconsistently and occasionally. This usually encourages the person to keep trying, checking or playing until they get what they want, without changing their own behavior.

The rewards associated with electronic slots might be in the form of cash, casino credits or prizes. In the case of your smartphone, they could include a new "like," friend, follower, non-spam text or even a phone call or voice message. Not always. Not every time. The addictive power of the intermittent reward is in its variability. Rewards are delivered enough to keep you engaged and coming back for more—in case the real-world attempts to distract you.

Tristan Harris, former Design Ethicist and Product Philosopher at Google, wrote an arresting essay called "How Technology Hijacks People's Minds—from a Magician and Google's Design Ethicist." His comments strongly support the similarities between electronic gaming devices and smartphones:

"Several billion people have a slot machine their pocket:

- When we pull our phone out of our pocket, we're playing a slot machine to see what notifications we got.
- When we pull to refresh our email, we're playing a slot machine to see what new email we got.
- When we swipe down our finger to scroll the Instagram feed, we're playing a slot machine to see what photo comes next.
- When we swipe faces left/right on dating apps like Tinder, we're playing a slot machine to see if we got a match.
- When we tap the number of red notifications, we're playing a slot machine to see what's underneath."

The similarities don't end there. According to Ms. Schüll, 80% of revenues in Las Vegas come from electronic machines rather than social forms of play around a table. Sociologically, human interaction with smartphones resembles that with electronic casino games. Though the user may be surrounded by other people, device interfaces have been designed to principally be used in isolation. The term "social media" may be something of an oxymoron.

Ms. Schüll also highlighted the ability to engage with electronic casino games continuously—with no need for a pause—as another hook into the psyche of the gambler:

Playing on slot machines is solitary, rapid and continuous. You don't have interruptions like you would in a live poker game, waiting for cards to be dealt or waiting for the other players. You can go directly from one hand to the next—there's no clear stopping point built into the game. You don't even have to stop to put bills in the machine; the machines take credit or barcoded tickets.

Mary Aiken, in *The Cyber Effect: A Pioneering Cyberpsychologist Explains How Human Behavior Changes Online*, wrote as it relates to the internet, "A combination of the fast delivery, exploring opportunities, unexpected information, and intermittent rewards create a medium that is enticing, exciting, and for some individuals totally irresistible." In your case, is your internet use merely compelling and important, or something more?

ARE YOU DISINHIBITED?

She also wrote that in cyberspace, "... we know that people may do and say things that they wouldn't do in the real-world ... for some, being in the cyber environment can impair judgment and increase impulsivity, somewhat similar to the way alcohol can. Disinhibition is facilitated by the environmental conditions of cyberspace—by the perceived lack of authority, the anonymity, as well as the sense of distance or physical remove."

Harvard University conducted a study on the addictiveness of social media from the perspective of its connection with pleasure. Eighty percent of our online conversations involve self-disclosure, compared to 30% to 40% in the real-world.

In the online context, we will say things about ourselves and others without the level of constraint that is socially appropriate in a face-to-face setting. In an online context, we can speak about ourselves in ways that give us pleasure, with no instant accountability for the truth or validity of what is said.

This is relevant because researchers have also concluded that disclosing information about oneself engages the brain in ways comparable with what occurs when you take an addictive substance. The research showed that pleasure centers triggered by eating, having sex or receiving money, were animated by speaking about oneself. This is especially true if the speaker knows that the details will be shared with others. Pleasure decreased perceptibly when the participants were told the information would not be shared with others.

DISTRACTION CAN BE DEADLY

Another indication of the compulsion associated with the internet is the inability to disconnect from it no matter the associated physical danger. The numbers of people dying as the result of distractions while driving, for example, or by getting into a position to capture just the right selfie, are rising.

Up to 80% of all vehicle crashes in the U.S. involve some form of driver distraction. One in four car accidents in the U.S., and nearly 330,000 of cell phone-related injuries are caused by *texting while driving*.

Striving to get an exceptional selfie also can be dangerous. The mortality rate connected with taking selfies has been doubling each year. Last year, thirty people died taking pictures of themselves with cell phones. And these were just the ones that were reported. These deaths involved falls, motor vehicles, electricity, drowning, firearms and more. A couple of examples:

- Two Russian soldiers in Siberia were posing for a selfie with a live grenade when it exploded. Only the phone with the photographic record of the event remained.
- A couple climbed over the safety barrier to a cliff in Cabo da Roca, Portugal. They took an unfortunate extra step backward to get just a bit better shot and fell to their deaths.

Whether it's a vehicle death while texting, striving to get a crazy selfie, or something else, these kinds of behaviors exemplify an excessive commitment to an online social presence. We want to be seen, among the hundreds of millions of social network members, as special in some way. Just as in the real-world, demonstrating uniqueness has become a tall and sometimes dangerous order.

Whether someone is hooked on alcohol, gambling or social media, one thing is almost always true: obsessive behavior leads to flawed assessments of the situational facts and circumstances. We run headlong into the worlds of new online friends and romantic interests that seem too good to be true. They may, of course, be fabulous. However, we are at a disadvantage in not being able to use our well-developed, real-world crap detectors, to test the appearance of perfection.

The more impulsive our actions, the less opportunity there is to recognize patterns from our experience that we can draw upon to be safer.

From a merely statistical perspective, the more time you spend online, the greater the odds you will encounter danger in one form or another. The more you keep your wits about you, the better chance you have of avoiding it or dealing with it appropriately.

THREE

CYBERSLACKERS: ONLINE COMPULSION GOES TO WORK

The difference between technology and slavery is that slaves are fully aware that they are not free.
~Nassim Nicholas Taleb

The intensity of our attraction to the online world can be problematic on our own time. But if we are not truly addicted, we should be able to get through a workday without checking in online. We should be able to leave the urge to surf at the door of our workplaces, true?

Not exactly. Whether you happen to be the boss or the employee (or both), most of us cannot resist the gravitational pull of cyberspace for a full workday—or even until the next official break. The requirements of work just can*not* be permitted to get in the way of dropping in on our now highly customized micro-asteroids in cyberspace.

WE'RE NOT NUMBER ONE

If you asked the average school-age child in the U.S., "What country in the world is the most productive?" the majority would immediately respond, "Ours of course! Who else?"

Each year, the World Economic Forum (WEF) ranks countries around the world against a most "productive and competitive" standard. Those measures seem to be tailor-made for the U.S. to perpetually top the list. However, in its most recent report, the WEF rated the U.S. the world's fifth most productive and competitive country, behind Switzerland, Singapore, Finland, and Germany.

The WEF concluded that, "As a nation develops, wages tend to increase and *labor productivity must improve*." (Emphasis added.) According to the U.S. Bureau of Labor Statistics, in the seven-year period ending in 2008, the average rise in per-employee productivity was about 2.3% per year. Since then, it has been roughly 1.3% per year. This may, in part, explain why the U.S. was not number one.

The Big Picture's Barry Ritholtz believes, and I agree, that "The way we capture formal productivity data hasn't kept up with modern ways of doing business ... Productivity models don't properly capture gains created by the application of new technology." However, even presuming the real rise in productivity is greater when factoring in the benefits from the integration of technology-based solutions, we are still not winning the productivity game. Consider some additional data.

CONNECTING WITH WHATEVER, WHENEVER, AND WHEREVER

A Harris Poll for CareerBuilder surveying 2,138 hiring and human resources managers as to the biggest workplace productivity killers, revealed that four of the top five are internet-related: cell phone, the Web, social media and non-work email use on the job. (The more traditional "engaging in office gossip" was also in the top five.) More than half of the employers surveyed reported that the biggest distraction at work came from employees using their cell phones, with 44% saying the same about using the internet.

According to a survey by International Data Corporation (IDC), 30% to 40% of internet access at the office is spent on non-work-related browsing. Other data indicate that 60% of all online purchases and 70% of pornographic website traffic occur during the nine to five workday hours (though not all access is made from a traditional workplace).

It goes on and on. Do you play, or know someone who pursues online "fantasy sports?" According to John Challenger, CEO of the global outplacement consultancy Challenger, Gray & Christmas, Inc., "Fantasy sports ranks with shopping ... and online poker as the biggest waste of productivity at the workplace." NFL Fantasy Football alone has a significant negative financial impact on the workplace. The group concluded that wages paid to workers last year while they were managing their NFL fantasy teams during business hours, approached $16 billion.

The same firm estimated that NCAA basketball March Madness last year cost employers about $4 billion in productivity. Some of this productivity drain occurred while workers kept track of the games and the office betting pool, certainly with some of that involving online resources.

The modest productivity growth rate of the American labor force is being chewed up, to a significant extent, by the use and abuse of internet access to social media and apps for non-work purposes. There is a unique and unflattering name for employees who abuse workplace internet access: cyberslackers.

If you run a small business or are self-employed, these issues and challenges exist as variations on the same themes. If you let non-work, online distractions eat up your day you are, in a very real sense, picking your own pocket.

THE PSYCHOLOGICAL EFFECT

Surveys of workers indicate many think that personal online exploration improves their productivity during the rest of the work day. Whether you believe this may depend on whether you are paying or receiving the compensation for the expected productivity. As with all such assessments, it is a matter of degree. Checking in with a friend online today probably equates to what, in the old days, might have been a ten-minute phone call or coffee break. Those kinds of interactions are positive if not pursued to excess, and they are something all of us do.

However, given the vastness of the cyberworld, and our devices' ability to instantly and ad infinitim deliver fresh content, it is easy to get sucked in. An hour later you look up and wonder where the time went. Now, you *really* need a break before returning to your work-work.

Even one lost hour per day, per employee, means an employer is paying one worker out of eight to be online full-time, pursuing non-work interests. How could this possibly enable the company to be more productive versus having eight employees who were just a little more efficient?

Considered another way, excessive on-the-job preoccupation with the internet and social media is destructive of the employment equation of "a fair day's wage for an honest day's work." In our heart of hearts, most of us have a sense of what that bargain means.

THE RULES — AND HOW TO GET AROUND THEM

About three-quarters of major U.S. companies keep tabs on employees by checking e-mail, internet use, phone records and computer files, or by videotaping them at work. Many organizations have written policies stating their position on using a company-supplied computer or smartphone for non-work purposes. Employers often restrict employee access to the internet or to specific websites, or they prohibit personal use of workplace computers and smartphones for non-work purposes altogether.

There is no universally recognized right to privacy for employees when it comes to employer monitoring or limiting of internet access or usage. In fact, 27% of companies indicate that they have successfully fired employees for misuse of office email or internet connections, and many have reported taking other disciplinary measures for those breaches.

But there is at least one way for employees to get around using workplace computers and networks. Roughly 95% of employees in businesses of all kinds use at least one personal device for their work. So even if a company has adopted policies regulating Web and social media use on work computers and smartphones, personal devices can eliminate the need for an employee to access business networks for non-work purposes.

Many larger businesses have closed this loophole by regulating the types of devices that can be brought into the workplace, and how they can be used once there. Given the small size and ubiquity of smartphones, such rules are almost impossible to enforce.

On the other hand, if personal device usage *is* permitted at work, employers can end up paying a high price. Allowing digital devices not monitored by or under the direct control of a company's IT team, comes with a cost. Blancco recently surveyed over 800 cybersecurity professionals to understand their mobile security challenges. One in five organizations reported suffering a mobile security breach because of malware and other intrusions brought in via employees' devices.

COMMON GROUND

Forrester wrote in a report about mobile devices, "The mobile mind shift is an expectation that an individual can get what he or she wants in their immediate context and moment of need." Cyberslackers might ask, "Why should it be any different at work?"

A partial answer is, of course, that an employee must perform at a level sufficient to keep the job. Excessive non-work use of the internet is a performance issue like any other.

On the other hand, given the ways in which the Web has become inextricably intertwined with our work and personal lives, we have reached a point of no return regarding internet use at work. In most businesses, online access cannot and should not be prohibited, but sanity must rule. Employees and employers must be realists when it comes to respecting the digital workplace. What's the common ground?

A good starting point would be an open, all-hands dialogue leading to a collective agreement to reduce cyberslacking. If that commitment can be met, it can lead to a shared victory: an improvement in the productivity of the organization, perhaps sufficient to enable the business to continue growing.

If the business remains on sound financial footing, there will be an ongoing need for workers, and the pay that goes with the status. Owners, shareholders, management *and* employees will reap the benefits, and we might even see rising American productivity as a by-product.

FOUR
A BILLION SOCIAL NETWORK DUPES AND FAKERS

I almost wish I hadn't gone down that rabbit-hole ...
~Alice, possibly referring to some of her online friends

Have you accepted online friends and connections with little or no vetting? If so, you may have invited total strangers to get an up-close-and-personal view of the details of your life.

Hundreds of millions of us are continuously connected and engaged in the pursuit of a wide variety of online social interactions. Many of us believe we can take what we know about real-world humanity—the paradigms of person-to-person authentication, trust, confidence, kindness and even the rule of law—and apply it to our sometimes compulsive and high-speed participation in the online social world.

Virtual social media communities count among their members almost three-quarters of all adults. There are over *twenty billion* registered accounts among the top tier social networking platforms (FaceBook, YouTube, Google+, etc.). Roughly half of them are categorized as "active," meaning that the account has been accessed within the past thirty days.

Because the Earth's current population is only about 7.4 billion, many users must be members of multiple social platforms, or something else is going on.

It's both.

MISTER ROBOT, TO YOU

More than half of Web traffic is made up of "bots," automated software programs that roam the net. Among these are spammers, scrapers, and other automated systems and hacking tools performing activities ranging from practical (background search functions, managing spreadsheets) to malicious (transporting computer viruses, shutting down sites, bombarding email inboxes with spam). These electronic denizens of the internet represent a good percentage of the neighbors in every social community of which you are a part.

As one example, last year a research report suggested that 8% of active Instagram accounts were spambots. Spambots create accounts and send spam messages. If there are 40,000,000 non-human spam delivery vehicles on Instagram with you, there is a good chance you might click on something hazardous to your digital health.

The spam messages you receive might be annoying but innocuous advertisements. They just as likely could contain links or attachments designed to tempt you. If you bite on them, you could be tricked into revealing personal information, or havoc could be wreaked on your digital device.

The bulk of remaining internet traffic is generated by humans—some trustworthy, some not so much. Among the legions of cyberfakers are real scammers, predators, trolls, and criminals, whose only objective is to steal your private information or shake you down in some other fashion.

Eliminating bad actors has become an enormous systemic challenge for all social network platforms and their valuable users, not just one unique to Facebook or Instagram.

CATFISH AND CONFIDENCE SCHEMES

The Web universe of the masked includes a broad spectrum of humanity. You might be contacted by a poor bastard who simply has a dull life, so he makes up a more exciting one and plays it out on the internet. If you make a connection with him, you have become a potential role player in his fake life.

A middle-aged guy from New York can portray himself as a college girl from Mississippi. No harm may be intended at the start, but real damage can result if the deception gains speed: bruised feelings, retaliatory stalking, ransom demands and more. (If you want to see examples of how this kind of trickery can impact lives in the real-world, watch a few episodes of the MTV reality show *Catfish*.)

In other cases, fake romantic relationships are instigated and vigorously pursued by scammers in distant countries. Often targeting the desperate and the elderly, these scams eventually coax the sending of money to the scammer for an "emergency," or as an advance of travel expenses for a visit to the victim that never takes place. There is an unlimited number of creative variations on this confidence scheme.

It doesn't even matter what network you're on. For example, because LinkedIn is designed as a business networking vehicle, more probity is often afforded its profiles and connection requests. It is, however, no different from networks like Facebook regarding scammers and fakers looking for victims.

Whatever the case, anonymity is the catalyst: fake names and photos, made-up accounts, false histories, gender impersonation and more. If you see some or all the following on any social or professional network, it may be a connection to avoid:

- The person is *too* photogenic. Or, if purportedly a woman, is wearing something inappropriately sexy or daring.
- Likewise, if the photo appears to be a high-quality stock photo, it is likely just what it seems: a false representation of the not-pictured man, woman or bot. There is no way to know.
- The person's current position doesn't seem to match the age indicated by the photo or presents an excessive title. "Global Managing Director, Ephemera—North America."
- Watch for banking positions and for social media and marketing executive positions.
- There is scant detail in the work history. There are gaps, or the employment history has just a few positions when more would make sense in the overall context of the profile.
- College names that aren't rational, or are overly generic. "Dorchester City College, Omaha, Nebraska." "Median University."

- The person has fewer than twenty connections. Probably, a "new account" looking for fast connections. How were you selected and why?
- Lower case letters where it would be normal to see capitals.
- If claiming to be an educated English speaker, the presence of odd and misplaced words, poor grammar and spelling.
- The profile owner location is not in the U.S., and it seems odd for the person in the photo to have located *you* "in all the world."
- If the profile is complete but appears to have been cut and pasted—it probably was.

The examples above are not fail-safe indicators of a bad actor, but they suggest more information is required to trust the connection.

If you mistakenly accept a connection that later seems to have been suspicious, immediately remove or block it. If you believe that connection is a person that could be a scammer, report it.

Whether you're on LinkedIn, Facebook, Google+ or another social networking site, be wary of an unlikely person, from a faraway place, contacting you out of the blue for no apparent reason.

SOCIAL CONGLOMERATES

The social networks with the greatest numbers of members are among the most recognized global brands today: Facebook, Twitter, LinkedIn, Pinterest, and Google+. In a recent thirty-day period, there were 170 million new downloads of apps for interacting with these and other platforms (including What'sApp, Facebook Messenger, Snapchat, Instagram, and YouTube).

At this pace, within just one year, these platforms alone could enable *two billion* access points for interaction with existing and new users. This is the unrelenting pace of growth in adopting today's social media and app platforms

None of the company brands mentioned above are based in China. It is the world's largest country, with a population of about

1.4 billion people. The Great Firewall of China, as the Chinese government's internet censorship project is commonly called, blocks Facebook, Twitter, Instagram and many other leading international social media players. China, of course, prefers its own versions of virtual social and messaging platforms and is currently serving an estimated 640 million members.

Most U.S. social networking platforms are publicly-held companies and must regularly file financial and other reports. The numbers are often hedged, qualified and shrouded in a haze of legalese. However, based upon the disclosures in these filings, most companies wouldn't contest that about 5% to 8% of their registered accounts are probably illegitimate, fakes or duplicates. If this assumption is correct, there are over a *billion* dupes and frauds of one kind or another on their registered membership rolls.

WHACK-A-MOLE

In the case of Facebook, for example, about 1.7 billion users are considered active every month. If you assume about 7% of active users are dupes or fake, this means roughly 119 million such users coexisting with you on Facebook. It could be even more. Facebook has publicly acknowledged that "Our data limitations may affect our understanding of certain details of our business."

Even if the Web population of intentional social network fakers is merely 320 million (the population of the United States), or only 8.55 million (the population of New York City), many social network friends and followers worthy of avoidance are present.

Although the number of fake accounts on social network platforms is huge, most of us bring a presumption of trust to our initial online interactions. In real-world face-to-face introductions, we typically go a little more slowly. But in our cyberworld, we tend to think that being behind a screen offers us invisibility. So, we embrace or at least overlook the potential consequences of letting virtual strangers into our lives. It is far too easy to (inappropriately) forsake our real-world caution, intuition and knowing in an online context.

This is an inappropriate transfer of our real-world knowing to an online context that is dissimilar in many ways. Many of us do this even though it cuts against what we believe about our personal online security. In fact, only 2% of adults believe they are "very secure" using social media communication to convey private information even to a *trusted* person or organization.

We acknowledge we are not secure online, but we connect anyway. "Damn the torpedoes, full speed ahead!" "While we're at it, hand me the blindfold too."

Even the best-run social networking platforms on the planet can't possibly know every individual in their base of members. Opening accounts, free or paid, is easy and involves virtually no vetting by the platform operators. For them, anything beyond the investigation of the most egregious offenders of the community regulations is an impossible game of Whack-A-Mole.

So, who or what—and how many—social network followers of the wrong kind have you authorized or even invited into your personal online world? Have your teens, parents, grandparents and others you care about been as careful as you have been?

If you don't know, I suggest you find out.

FIVE

ANYTHING YOU SHARE MAY BE USED AGAINST YOU

*****

To paraphrase a notable quotation:
"Being a little paranoid is appropriate when your
worst fears could come true with a single click."

Why is it so important to be aware of who your friends and followers are on social media? For one thing, these are the people (and non-human bots) who can see anything and everything you post.

Are you among those inclined to post where you're going for dinner and with whom, or your vacation destination and how long you'll be away? Such a voluntary "share" also advises criminals where you and your companions *won't* be. Potential burglars are delighted for you to make their work a little easier by including them among your followers. The question is whether the value of those kinds of posts—shared with *anyone*—is worth the potential of a highly personal, and negative, intrusion into your real-life.

Five of the top ten fears cited by the respondents in last year's "Chapman University Survey of American Fears" were related to our interactions with the online world: cyberterrorism, corporate tracking of personal information, government tracking of personal data, identity theft and credit card fraud. This year, all but one of those cyber fears (corporate tracking) remained in the top twenty.

Despite these pervasive societal threats, we regularly and voluntarily provide the precise data we say we are concerned about revealing. In other words, *our* online behaviors are often the cause of our fears being realized.

Most social media platforms (and many other sites) require disclosure of some amount of personal information. Over half of the users share their dates of birth, the names of their family members and their school names. Other commonly shared information includes relationship status, hometown, employment information, vacation plans and at least some data on connections and followers. Many sites also require a credit card or banking information.

These bits of information, when stitched together, can be used to create a partial or even complete profile of your identity. This is the "data fingerprint" mentioned in Chapter One, You've Been Hacked. The more complete the profile, the more valuable it is for spambots, cybercriminals and others thriving on the underbelly of social media. The negative consequences of sharing can include identity theft, fraud, reputational attacks and damage, real-world threats like burglary and stalking, and cyberbullying.

Another consequence—not threatening but still intrusive and irritating—is your receipt of advertising more precisely targeted for you (or actually, "at you"). The operators of social networks generate revenue—a lot of it—with customized advertising based on the specific personal information you provide. The more exact targeting is not just a result of the data you provide at initial enrollment. After visiting websites offering certain products and services, have you seen comparable offers in the context of other Web pages, or in your Facebook feed? The level of awareness of "what you are thinking about" that seems to be following you is not random nor accidental.

As mentioned in Chapter One, McAfee.com calls personal data the "oil" of the digital economy. "The commercial market for personal data is booming, with large databases of subscriber information driving up the enormous valuations of those [social media] companies that own it." It will not surprise you that the higher the number of monthly active users reported, the more money the social platform companies make. Why? Three out of four consumers rely on social media to influence purchasing decisions, and advertisers know it. Better targeting means a greater degree of success per dollar spent generating demand.

YOU SHARED WHAT?

* * * * * * *

Social networks have evolved as places where what used to be considered extreme full disclosure is now merely being friendly. In the U.S., about 77% of adults post on social media and share content, often personal. We apparently want to share, and we also are directly and subliminally encouraged to share, because it has a positive effect on the revenue and marketing power of the social media companies. Facebook has the largest user base, and Statista reported that 57% of global content sharing activity occurs on their platform.

One route to overexposure is posting something rather personal on a good friend's page. But then, if you have two-hundred Facebook friends, they will all potentially be made aware of it. Depending on privacy settings and other factors, *their* friends and possibly even complete strangers can also see it. Perhaps the best question to ask is, "Do I care if any or all of this information was in the hands of someone that wanted to hack my personal life?"

Active sharing is one thing, but the accidental release of confidential personal information can also have adverse consequences. Another Statista survey revealed that due to unwitting disclosure, 25% of users had suffered some loss of personal reputation, 20% had lost friends, 17% said it led to bullying or harassment, and 15% indicated they had suffered financial losses.

Interestingly, during the past eighteen months or so, there has been a downshift in public sharing on social platforms. It could be that the drumbeat of announcements of data breaches has awakened social network members to the dangers of oversharing.

It might also be attributed to the rise in awareness that users are giving more than they are getting. "The more Facebook feels like a big stage, the less inviting it becomes to the sorts of people who aren't comfortable performing in public—which is to say, most of us," writes Jeff Bercovici for *INC. Magazine*. It could be both. Bercovici continued, "I used to be one of these annoying Facebook exhibitionists. Then, six months ago, my account got hacked, and I spent several painful days recovering it. Since then, my relationship with Facebook has changed…"

FEND FOR YOURSELF

Even if they wanted to—and could *afford* to—social network platform companies cannot protect you from contact with fakers and other bad apples. How many social network moderators would it take to stay on top of even just the most compelling complaints about an aggressive or annoying intrusion? How many law enforcement investigators and police officers would be required to monitor, let alone investigate, all such alleged offenses? Law enforcement agencies already have their hands more than full with real-life bad actors.

You, your friends, children, parents, co-workers and social acquaintances are always just one click away from a scammer, stalker, predator, pedophile or another social media sewer dweller. Sometimes these are real people (though it would be almost impossible to physically locate them), but many times they are simply digital robots.

As noted in the previous chapter, these bots are continuously unleashed for commercial purposes. They can appear as new friends and connections for you to add to your profile, and might help raise your social media "score." Some, though, are merely trying to get a hook into your digital world to exploit you. Which ones?

Even for those individuals who are barely seen, hardly followed and little-liked on social networks, there is a measure of online risk that requires constant vigilance. The greater your presence on social media, the more visible you can make your whereabouts, your stuff, the private parts of your body and the details of your life. This, of course, can directly lead to a greater number of followers of the wrong kind.

If you take away only one thing from this book, I hope it is this: In navigating the unique cyberuniverse you have created, your inappropriate trust and oversharing of personal information, *must* be replaced with a modicum of caution and your best, independent judgment.

The best way to protect your own reputation is *before* the genie is out of the bottle. What doesn't get posted or shared then doesn't have to be managed after-the-fact. If you have any doubt about content you are considering posting, ask a trusted friend to give you a sanity check before doing so. Pause before you click yourself into an abyss.

KEEPING UP WITH KIM

* * * * * * *

The star power of highly recognizable people in the real-world is magnified in the cyberworld. Exhibit A is Kim Kardashian, the Mother-of-All-Social-Media.

Based on her success, it appears that almost everyone has something to learn from her about monetizing social media. She, her nuclear Kardashian family, and her Jenner sisters (Kendall and Kylie) collectively have more than 500 million social media followers among just Twitter, Facebook, and Instagram.

Ms. Kardashian has taken the public exposure of private moments to a never-before-seen level. One Monday morning, she tweeted a full-frontal selfie sans clothing to her Kardashian Nation. Bette Midler saw it and tweeted in response, @bettemidler "Kim Kardashian tweeted a nude selfie today. If Kim wants us to see a part of her we've never seen, she's gonna have to swallow the camera."

This comment by Ms. Midler may have been an oblique reference to the fact that Kardashian got her start with a privately videotaped sexual encounter that later became public. Today, not only is Kim Kardashian the leading figure in mainstream social media globally, but the sex tape that started it all is the most-viewed online porn video year in and year out.

Kim Kardashian (now) West has also authored a best-selling book entitled *Selfish*, composed entirely of "selfies," presumably for those who missed them the first time she posted them online. There is also a new version of the book appropriately entitled *More Me!*

Ms. Kardashian's massive follower population can read her beauty secrets and random, earnest bits of borrowed wisdom. They can see family photos, another opening night event of something fabulous, her amazing jewelry, and witness her attempts to "break the internet" with photos of her impressive backside. She is exploiting her position and followers for an estimated $50 million a year in income, and who can blame her? Fame, glamor, globetrotting, Kanye-the-Great, kids named North and Saint, and lots and lots of pure adoration—she has reached social media nirvana.

In addition to her earning power and celebrity—or perhaps because of it—she is the object of public ridicule, hate speech, predators, stalkers, and criminals. Her standing exemplifies the double-edged sword that is social media. Given her number of followers, her willing objectification of her looks and body, the public flaunting of her children, her entertainer-celebrity husband, and her wealth, she is one of the most tempting targets for the infliction of online and real-world malice.

On a Fashion Week trip to Paris, Ms. Kardashian was assaulted one day, mobbed by paparazzi the next and, on a third, robbed inside her Parisian hotel room by two armed men dressed as police officers. Many reports at the time indicated that Kardashian was gagged, handcuffed and, with her feet bound, held at gunpoint in a bathtub.

In the end, she wasn't physically hurt, but she suffered the loss of some jewelry and her phone. For most of us, this would be aggravating and inconvenient. In her case, though, the ring had an estimated value of $4.5 million. She had Snapped a photo of it for her followers (and apparently, the robbers were among them) earlier in the week. The rest of her jewelry was worth about $7 million. Not your ordinary purse snatching.

As you would expect, Ms. Kardashian has the best social media managers, moderators, and online safety and protection that money can buy. She also has the extra layer of bodyguard protection. But when you seek that level of visibility in everything you do, there is no place to hide. After the Paris incident, she hired people once responsible for protecting the President of the United States—former Secret Service agents. Hopefully, they will be able to keep up with her and ensure her physical safety. The redoubled efforts will no doubt involve some monitoring of her online activity to better anticipate and minimize potential threats.

ONE LESS SELFIE

Could there be a silver lining to her experience? Given her extreme exposure and the pain of the ordeal she suffered personally, it might be possible for her to turn it into a cautionary tale for her social media followers. As a supplement to selfies and advertising (masquerading as beauty tips), what if Ms. Kardashian were to offer a daily tip as to how girls and women can better be safe and secure in online social communities? What if she harnessed her enormous Web influence in the cause of identifying and reducing the number of deceptions and threats to naïve social network users of all genders and ages?

In fact, *anyone* with a significant social media presence could help by spreading this kind of awareness. Even if Ms. Kardashian alone joined with the executives of some of the major social network communities to change the cyberworld for the better, over a half a billion people could be influenced to be more aware and cautious when using social media platforms.

These actions could have a substantial and rapid impact on reducing cyber-social behavior that goes over the line. Kardashian's efforts could influence people to think twice before oversharing online.

Who knows? Maybe educating the public on the importance of greater awareness in navigating social media could even result in some bling of a different kind: humanitarian awards.

SIX
YOUR ONLINE REPUTATION PRECEDES YOU

* * * * *

Whether you know it or not, there is very likely something about you "Now Showing" online.

If you happen to be one of the 25% of Americans who has never searched your name, or if you haven't done so in a while, please do it now. Just type your name into the Google, Bing or Yahoo search box, take a deep breath and click.

It is possible, though increasingly unlikely, that the search results return nothing at all. You could discover that you share your name with a heroic historical figure in Ireland, a heart surgeon in Connecticut or, on the darker side, a murderer in New Mexico. Or if you have a common name, like "John Smith," the references to your life may be buried under results relating to another, more famous John Smith.

It could be that the results of your search only include a reference to your Facebook or LinkedIn account. Perhaps your name is associated with a local newspaper account celebrating your good deeds, a photo of you completing a half-marathon, or the specifics of political contributions you have made. Or, you could find an unwelcome reminder of a temporary loss of judgment one evening twenty years ago (hopefully on page 17 of the search results).

Right or wrong, your best or worst foot forward is likely first presented online.

Most online mentions have some reputational effect, positive or negative. Harris Interactive recently conducted a survey on behalf of BrandYourself.com asking 2,570 American adults about their search habits. Of those who had previously searched their name, 48% indicated they considered the results to be negative. Many survey respondents indicated they have searched for the name of the person they are meeting on a first date. Of those, about half found something that made them decide not to follow through with it; the other half saw something that affirmed their decision to go.

You are likely aware that it is common practice for employers to scour the Web for background on potential hires, but you may not know how common the practice is. The online reputation management company ReputationX.com reports that "75% of U.S. companies have formal policies requiring recruiters to research job applicants online, and 70% of U.S. recruiters and hiring managers have rejected candidates based on information found online." Gainful employment may depend on a positive online reputation.

If anonymity is your preference, there's some good news. Each month well over *a hundred billion* Web searches are conducted, most of which obviously have no connection to you. So even if a search of your name returns results with which you're unhappy, you are a very, very tiny needle in an enormous haystack. But, if you don't stay on top of what happens when someone searches your name, something negative may first be brought to your attention by someone close to you—whether at work or home.

In addition to your relative online invisibility, there is more good news. Ninety percent of Google traffic is generated by the first page of search returns. Only 75% of users scroll past the first page, and far fewer go beyond the second. Lori Randall Stradtman, author of *Online Reputation Management for Dummies*, asks with tongue firmly in cheek: "Where do you hide a dead body? On the third page of Google results."

EXTORTION IS A CLICK AWAY

Even if there are just a few mentions of you in current online search results, there are more serious potential issues that can land on your head. TrendMicro annually identifies significant cyber issues and trends. They identified this as the "Year of Online Extortion." They predicted, "Attackers will continue to use fear" as their main tool. "Cyber extortionists will devise new ways to target a victim's psyche to make each attack 'personal'—either for an end user or an enterprise." A wide variety of specific malware (referred to as "ransomware") is deployed as a means to extort cash from victims fearing for their online and real-life reputations.

For example, shaking down someone with an active interest in pornography represents one of the easiest online ransom opportunities. Last year, over 4.4 billion hours of online porn were viewed during 21.2 billion site visits globally. Of this, 41% was attributed to viewers located in the U.S., where an estimated $10 billion a year is spent on "adult entertainment."

According to the TrendMicro report, ransomware can be planted on a user's system as a consequence of them clicking an ad or another link when visiting an online porn site. Once infected, a message may appear on the screen indicating it is from law enforcement and that the device has been frozen because it was used to view pornography. The message might claim that child pornography was found on the computer, even if this isn't true. Typically, the victim will be told he must pay or face arrest and be outed publicly.

Although porn viewership is huge, most individuals understandably prefer to keep their usage private. Having their name come up in search results as a "porn addict," "distributor of child pornography," or worse, is highly undesirable. Therefore, many victims prefer to pay a ransom to avoid such exposure and the potential for reputational damage. Once paid, the victim's hope is that their first payment is their last. Often, that's not the end of it.

If this or any other damaging information appears about you in search results, it may be necessary to contact Google or another search engine provider and ask that the unfavorable content and link be taken down. (https://support.google.com/Websearch/answer/2744324)

Of course, it's not always easy. You can *ask,* but Google and others will not always agree to act. And there are often many layers you might need to dig through. For example, if the information you wish to have removed has been sourced from a website other than Google, you will need to directly contact that website and request its removal.

As mentioned above, about 75% of Americans have Googled their name to see what comes up. But fewer than 20% make an effort to proactively monitor their online presence and reputation on an ongoing basis. That is, until information damaging to their reputation appears in an online mention. When negative results appear, 77% of those experiencing such pain, get religion about online reputation monitoring. Why wait for that kind of unpleasant wake-up call?

THE DOOR TO YOUR BUSINESS IS THROUGH THE WEB

The barriers to cross-border online commerce have fallen. Appearing credible and well-presented online has become a critical success factor for businesses of all sizes. If you own and operate a smaller business, both your *personal and business* names will commonly be checked out in advance. If the online presentation is poor, in most cases you won't even know that a potential customer has walked away.

Here are some statistics provided by ReputationX.com illustrating why no matter how small your business, it is important to proactively manage its online reputation:

- 65% of internet users see online search as the most trusted source of information about people and companies.
- 79% of consumers place equal weight on online reviews and personal recommendations.
- Nearly 97% of consumers say they read online reviews about local businesses.

What appears online, and doesn't, can make or break your business. And you can't avoid the issue. If you own or operate a business and you have *no* online presence, that fact is reason enough for many potential customers to look for another provider of your goods or services. If you are listed in directories like Yelp, Angie's List or something similar, and no one has yet posted a review of your business, it may appear that "nobody's home." It doesn't take much effort to give your small business a fighting chance with a positive online presence.

REPUTATION MANAGEMENT

* * * * * * *

For those willing to pay for the service of monitoring and managing search results, there are many businesses now dedicated to this. The majority are focused on business reputation monitoring and shaping, but a number also address personal reputation management. One example of the latter, with a strong focus on Google results, is www.brandyourself.com. Here are a couple of links where you can compare numerous providers of these kinds of services: http://www.topseos.com/rankings-of-best-reputation-management-companies and http://www.toptenreviews.com/business/marketing/best-online-reputation-management-services/

Whether you have acknowledged this reality before now, your reputation is front and center on Google and other search engines. Your online and real-world reputations are already intertwined. You can be confident that friends, acquaintances, prospective customers, potential employers and romantic interests, will at some point search to see what they can find out about you. Why not make it your personal responsibility to put your best foot forward? It is, you know.

SEVEN

CYBERCRIME PAYS

*"Man is least himself when he talks in his own person.
Give him a mask, and he will tell you the truth."*
~Oscar Wilde

The saying "Crime doesn't pay" doesn't apply in the online world. It pays well, and cybercriminals are difficult to catch. It doesn't take much technical aptitude to get into the trade; current tools, products, how-to manuals, and services make it pretty easy to get into the saddle.

The internet's explosive expansion and anonymity have created a worldwide electronic haven from which cybercriminals can work. All the potential criminal opportunities available in the real-world remain in the digital age. Plus, there is a whole new smorgasbord of computer-, smartphone-, and internet-enabled and enhanced crimes from which online criminals can choose.

The Oscar Wilde quotation above might be updated to read, "Humans are more easily judged face-to-face. Behind a screen, they will deceive you if it serves their purposes." Consider the advantages of having a mask, or a protective shield, between yourself and everyone else—hidden, yet able to inflict harm at will.

UNTOUCHED BY HUMAN HANDS

Cybercriminals don't have to be near a potential victim to accomplish what they want. They don't have to be in the same city, country or even hemisphere. They don't have to look the potential victim in the eye or physically confront them. They don't even have to leave their office, cyber café or beach chair.

Time and resources can be conserved by using a "one-to-many" model: reaching numerous potential victims using a single scheme that can be carried out over the course of a few seconds, minutes or hours. In financial terms, this represents what is known as a scalable business model.

Anonymity in cyberspace is still virtually unlimited. It just takes a digital device, an internet connection, and a good scheme, to launch oneself as an online criminal. There is at best only a small probability that a cybercriminal can be physically located, let alone investigated, prosecuted or incarcerated. This is not an overstatement. I offer these facts with the intention of raising your awareness that your knowledge of online safety practices, along with the exercise of good judgment, are essential for keeping you and yours out of harm's way.

CYBERCRIME FIGHTING

Drawing from all the different definitions of cybercrime, Symantec defines it as "Any crime that is committed using a computer network or hardware device." At a high level, the laws and regulations relating to cybercrime typically address the following:

- Improper access to, or interference with, a network or another person's computer or device.
- The theft of data or information.
- The introduction of a virus or other malware into a computer system.
- The use of a computer to perpetrate a fraud on another person or entity.

Let's look just at the impact of malware (malicious software). AppRiver LLC, a leading provider of email, messaging and Web security solutions, recently reported that "Malware attacks are on the upswing, coming at a rate that is close to four times last year. During a recent three-month period, we recorded 4.2 billion malicious emails and 3.35 billion spam emails. Meanwhile, there were 43 million unique Web-borne threats daily ..." Presuming each of the referenced actions was reported, where would an investigation begin in pursuit of the perpetrators of so many attacks?

Cyber investigations are now handled by nearly every law enforcement agency, from Homeland Security investigations to local police departments. Last year, Congress authorized the FBI to hire about 2,000 additional agents, with the intention that many would be assigned to fight cybercrimes.

(On a side note, the current FBI Director has said it has become harder to hire hackers to tackle cybercrime due to their use of marijuana. Current agency regulations won't accept employees who have smoked pot in the past three years. This apparently leaves a lot of otherwise qualified applicants out of the candidate pool.)

Cybercriminals from every corner of the globe take advantage of the anonymity of the Web to hide from authorities. Imagine the complexity and expense of fully policing cyberspace and doing it cooperatively across national borders. As a global community, we often cannot even agree where to be seated at negotiating tables, let alone how to cooperatively address highly complex issues relating to cybercrime.

Many still developing countries have not yet adopted laws addressing cybercrime. It is no coincidence that such countries are host to significant global online criminal enterprises. These organizations are sometimes run by teens and young adults, using rent-by-the-hour computers in cyber cafes. They live in places where the opportunities are few, and they have little to lose.

In the real-world, the structures and processes of investigation and law enforcement have evolved slowly, changing and maturing over the years. Understanding and applying these models has made the real-world investigative process more predictable and efficient.

Such investigations are often triggered by the discovery of physical evidence. The man's head is bleeding. The money is missing. The victim is not breathing. Consequently, law enforcement assesses real-world crime scenes with a standard set of investigative processes based in physical reality. Dusting for fingerprints, taking hair from a brush, checking surveillance video, etc.

This is just as true in cyberspace. Mary Aiken, Ph.D., writes in *The Cyber Effect*, "Almost everything we do online generates digital exhaust, digital dust, and digital prints. This digital evidence can help law enforcement investigate criminal behavior." However, electronic crime scenes are also dynamic, not static. Computers and smartphones can be destroyed, IP addresses changed or faked. Posts and evidence of threats made can be removed.

There are tens of millions of cybercrime victims each year, and online criminal enterprises are running at the speed of the internet. How could law enforcement processes and procedures based in the real-world possibly keep up with the scale, speed and diversity of cybercrime? Currently, there are far fewer cybercops than there are electronic crime scenes to investigate. Many law enforcement officers are untrained in cyberinvestigation techniques.

Although progress is being made, a comprehensive, global approach to Web rules and enforcement is still a very long way out. Just like "social media," the term "Web regulation" remains, at least for now, a bit of an oxymoron.

There is no doubt that you must access the Web and social communities for the vast resources and content they contain. On the other hand, as Dorothy said, "Toto, I've a feeling we're not in Kansas anymore." Be aware that once online, the place and the game have changed.

DON'T MAKE IT ANY EASIER

As previously discussed, cybercrime attacks on individuals are typically a consequence of personal information that is publicly disclosed. This exposure could result from a data breach at a company (Yahoo and Target are examples), through malicious links or attachments in emails or on the Web, or through your own sharing of bits and pieces of personal information.

Once supplied to a financial institution, merchant or even government, the privacy of your data fingerprint is subject to their planning, protection, and continuing diligence. The vast majority of companies will do the best they can to prevent and defend your data. It is never in their best commercial interests to put their customers at risk if they can possibly prevent it.

Yet day in and day out, business data breaches are growing in size and frequency. It is inevitable that you will be a secondary victim of such a large-scale breach if you haven't been already.

More and more breaches go undiscovered, at least for several months if not longer. As we have seen, the personal data of over 500 million Yahoo customers had been compromised for over two years before a formal acknowledgment was made by the company.

In its latest Internet Security Threat Report, Symantec suggested that it is now an accepted practice for businesses to not disclose breaches at all. "The total reported number of exposed identities [last year] jumped 23 percent to 429 million. But this number hides a bigger story … Companies choosing not to report the number of records lost increased by 85%."

A decision by a company to hide or delay releasing information about the exposure of customers' personal data, seems to be entirely and inappropriately self-interested. It is a choice made to preserve a positive brand reputation and retain customers. It is ironic that many providers of goods and services will choose to leave their customers in the dark after their personal data has been compromised. Hopefully, legislation will address this obscene consumer exploitation. Data breaches like Yahoo's and others are bad situations made worse through nondisclosure to those affected. We deserve better.

IT'S ON YOU

* * * * * *

Over 80% of users report they would feel devastated if their personal financial information was compromised. Almost half of users report feeling furious after learning they have become a victim of an online breach or other cybercrime. Despite these feelings, we are less than industrious in our efforts to protect ourselves and our data fingerprint information.

A Norton survey found that many people do not even have passwords or PINs on their devices, and if they do, they are often shared. This is something that can and must change. Hopefully, your reading of *CYBERCRISIS* will provide the stimulus to at least use and keep private your passwords and PINs.

In fact, most of the responsibility for online privacy protection falls on you. There is no silver bullet product, tool, or go-to person to whom you can offload it. Continuous awareness, consistent use of preventive and protective tools and actions (starting with strong passwords), and ongoing curiosity about cyberspace—these are the essentials of an online security plan.

Cybercrime threats are personal, and there are none more personal than online scams. In such cases, the perpetrator works to gain the confidence of the targeted victim, and then exploits it. The form and execution of such schemes are only limited by the creativity of the cybercriminal. It is a topic worthy of exploration at a level not possible in this work. For our purposes, a good start for improving your knowledge about and recognition of internet scams is reading the FBI descriptions of the most common ones. Learn about them by checking out the FBI's Internet Crime Complaint Center website.

Who should care more than you about protecting yourself at a basic level? Better online protection doesn't require you to have more knowledge than what's readily accessible to you through just another Web search. Another starting point for the basics, is the information in Chapters Nine and Ten.

Even if you aren't motivated to learn and implement online security basics for yourself, you are probably responsible for others: children, students, co-workers, friends, and parents. Do it for them, and for all of those who cannot protect themselves online as readily as you can.

A four-year-old texting is adorable, but she doesn't yet know about online threats and how to protect herself. Yet, because you gave a smartphone to her with internet access enabled, she holds in her hands a two-way connection with those on the other side of her screen. For some cybersafety tips for younger children, take a look at this site: http://www.safekids.com/kids-rules-for-online-safety/

The internet is, in many ways, still a frontier. Law and order are on the way, and ultimately will be up to the challenge. As of now, however, cyberspace remains the new "Old West, " and unfortunately, ripe for the picking of the online innocent, uninitiated and unprotected.

EIGHT

THE HIDDEN WEB

* * * * *

Although many believe the "internet" and the "Web" are the same, technically speaking these are not interchangeable terms.

The internet is a physical network infrastructure including connected computers and digital devices. When we connect to the internet, we are literally linking our device to a global network. In doing so, our device becomes part of the internet until we disconnect it.

The Web, on the other hand, refers to the content that is built to utilize the information superhighway that is the internet. The Web also encompasses the communication protocols that allow the sharing of data: files, Web pages, images, and much more content. When we search for and view these things, we are exploring the Web. Or at least *part* of it.

In our daily Web journeys, we typically access only what is known as the Visible Web (or Surface or Clear Web). This is mainly because it is so well-organized and instantaneously responsive. The content of the Visible Web is continuously organized by major search engine providers such as Google, Bing, Yahoo! Search, Baidu (China), and many others using standard practices. This structured method of cataloging content enables Web exploration via a browser and search terms that rapidly yield results in the form of links.

The letters and numbers that make up a link are collectively known as the "uniform resource locator" (URL) or Web address. They represent the location of information on the internet. You click on the link and the page you're requesting instantly appears on your screen for viewing.

This indexed portion of the Web, though huge (4.82+ billion pages), is only a small fraction of the information and content that make up the Web. If you think of the entirety of the Web as an iceberg, the Hidden or Invisible Web (more commonly referred to as the Deep Web) is below the "water line." And within the Deep Web lies the even more forbidding-sounding Dark Web.

THE DEEP WEB

The term Deep Web refers to the unindexed part of the internet. Because it isn't as organized as the Visible Web, it is mostly *in*visible to everyday users. Its pages cannot be reached using conventional search methods.

Much of Deep Web content is somewhat "dry." It includes databases of information from government departments and agencies such as the I.R.S., Social Security Administration, NASA and the U.S. Patent and Trademark Office. There is also much information from the internal networks of companies and universities. In the case of most Web users, directly accessing Deep Web content is not crucial nor worth the effort.

However, you indirectly access Deep Web content virtually every day. When you log in to your email account, online bank account, or Amazon account, you're using the Deep Web. In fact, about ninety-five per cent of Deep Web content is information that underlies Visible Websites.

A few sites that access Deep Web data relating to the travel industry, include Expedia, Travelocity, Hotwire, and Airbnb. As a service, these companies and many similar Web portals (aggregators and organizers of specialty content), drill into the data underlying the Web sites of multiple hotels and airlines, and package up the results for your immediate viewing.

If you have an interest, or if it supports your requirements for research, Deep Web content can be accessed directly through select browsers, the best-known of which is called The Onion Router. Commonly referred to as TOR, its full name reflects a design that can obscure data and identities under multiple layers of encryption. If used correctly and with the right associated tools, TOR permits anonymous access and exploration of the Deep Web, even by the not-so-technically inclined.

If that sounds like too much work, but you're still interested in getting a taste for the Deep Web, look at Hidden Wiki. https://thehiddenwiki.org/ This is a wiki page that catalogs some of the Deep Web's key websites.

YOUR HACKED DATA HAS BEEN FOUND... ON THE DARK WEB

The Dark Web is identified as a part of the Deep Web, but it is only a tiny fraction of its size. The TOR browser mentioned above can also be used for exploration of Dark Web sites. When properly configured and managed, you can access Dark Web content without disclosing your identity, location, your computer's IP address and other information typically used for tracking. I would not recommend exploring the Dark Web, but if you are interested, I strongly suggest that initially you do so with a knowledgeable guide.

The Dark Web is sometimes described as a shadowy underground marketplace, a "black market." Hackers and cybercriminals from all around the world use its anonymity and additional protections to make it virtually impossible to track or identify them.

As mentioned in previous chapters, much of the value in hacked data is turning it into cash. The Dark Web is considered the internet's "Hacked Data Depository." McAfee writes, "As the commercial value of personal data grows, cybercriminals have long since built an economy selling stolen data to anybody with a computer browser and the means to pay." Stolen personal, health and financial information, hacking for hire services, spam and phishing campaigns, and a whole lot more (see below) are offered on the Dark Web.

In an extensive article in Vanity Fair, William Langewiesche writes, "The real action on the Dark Net is in the trade of information. Stolen credit cards and identities, industrial secrets, military secrets, and especially the fuel of the hacking trade: the zero days and back doors that give access to closed networks." Fundamentally, it consists of the places online where you would not want your information to appear at all, and certainly not for sale. However, in the wake of data breaches, your name, address, bank and credit card account numbers and other detailed information could end up available for sale there.

As referenced above, McAfee Labs published a report titled "The Hidden Data Economy." Some of the specific findings will open your eyes to the importance of protecting your data fingerprint with more vigilance. Yet they also reveal how little that data is worth on its own:

- Average estimated price for stolen credit and debit cards: $5 to $30 in the United States; $20 to $35 in the United Kingdom; $20 to $40 in Canada; $21 to $40 in Australia; and $25 to $45 in the European Union.
- Bank login credentials for a $2,200 balance bank account, selling for $190.
- Bank login credentials plus stealth funds transfer to U.S. banks, priced from $500 for a $6,000 account balance to $1,200 for a $20,000 account balance.
- Online payment service login credentials priced between $20 and $50 for account balances from $400 to $1,000; between $200 and $300 for balances from $5,000 to $8,000.

(from BGR.com)

As reported by RSA, a provider of cybersecurity systems, the sheer number of hacked personal accounts has driven the prices for other parts of your identity way down. Here is a look at some recent offers on the Dark Web:

- A social media account with more than 500 friends: $5.00
- Retailer account credentials (relative value determined by the retailer, the age of the account, and if it has a credit card attached): $2.00 to $10.00

- False identification documents: English $15.00, Spanish $13.00–$15.00, French and Italian $10.00

The real value of these personal assets, when sold, is in the multiplier effect. Five dollars is a mere five dollars. But when you multiply it times a thousand it becomes a much more attractive proposition for the cyberthief.

A report from Terbium Labs, "Separating Fact from Fiction: The Truth About the Dark Web," says about fraudsters utilizing your hacked personal data, "Dark Web vendors have thoroughly systematized the fraud trade, offering everything from bank drops (bank accounts) to fullz (full identities) to credit cards or music-streaming credentials ... On the more sophisticated carding markets, [potential purchasers] can sort and filter by bank, card type, city, state, issuer—a host of different options to narrow down a specific set of cards for purchase."

The Terbium report also cautions that "... many of the most prolific fraud sites technically are a part of the Surface Web. These sites often operate on top level domains based in countries less likely to shut down sites hosting illegal activity. Some of these include domains tied to Western Samoa (.ws), Cameroon (.cm), Cocos Islands (.cc), and Oman (.om)." In poker terms, these two letters at the end of the URL represent a "tell," something that provides a clue that deserves special notice. At the very least, your antennae should rise if you find yourself on a site with a domain other than the most common ones, such as .com, .org, .gov, .edu, and so on.

ON SALE, TODAY ONLY:
ALL CYBERCRIME PRODUCTS AND SERVICES

* * * * * * *

"The [Dark Web] has evolved to include almost every conceivable cybercrime product for sale or rent," according to "The Hidden Data Economy," the previously referenced research report issued by McAfee. They write that their project took them to underground sites describing offers to "... commit murder for hire. For $45,000, a hit man, offering 'professionalism,' would murder someone upon request. Targets in the public eye would cost $180,000. Apparent hit men also offer crippling, bombings, making a person 'go missing,' and 'simple' beatings of individuals or entire families." (Other researchers conclude that some or many such sites may be fakes or run by undercover law enforcement officials.)

TrendMicro, writing about cybercrime and other digital threats, called out other offerings available on the Dark Web, including "... selling contraband like drugs and firearms ... supplying child pornography ... online extortion, identity theft, digital vandalism, and even cyber-terrorism ..." Silk Road was the most well-known example of an online marketplace selling illegal drugs. Users were able to browse and purchase anonymously. Silk Road was the creation of Ross Ulbricht, who was arrested by the FBI in San Francisco in 2013 and later sentenced to life in prison without parole for his cybercrimes.

Though illicit and anonymous, once there you will find that the Dark Web is a real commercial marketplace with multiple vendors of similar products and services. There certainly is an element of competition. Some sellers offer discount days, coupon codes, two-for-one specials, money-back guarantees and loyalty points. Some offer to provide refunds for purchased stolen credit cards if declined at a retailer.

Because there are user ratings and references, drugs sold over the Dark Web tend to be higher quality and therefore safer than those sold face-to-face. In fact, drugs dominate the illegal content on the Dark Web, so vendors have a reason to care about distinguishing themselves. Some post comments so that potential purchasers can read firsthand about the experiences of satisfied customers. In its report, Terbium cited the instance of a vendor commenting on one buyer's meth review. "You can tell what type of battery provided the acid used to cook a batch of meth. One brand is said to 'lend a taste of lime, coffee, and cigar.'" An idea, perhaps, for a Dark Web cooking show.

The research report mentioned above by Terbium Labs offers the view that a significant percentage of the content of Dark Web sites is entirely legal. The report states that "Tor Hidden Services play host to Facebook, European graphic design firms, Scandinavian political parties, personal blogs about security, and forums to discuss privacy, technology, even erectile dysfunction. Anonymity does not equate criminality, merely a desire for privacy. Just because much of the content is legal, though, doesn't mean it's safe. Legal content has the potential to be damaging, even dangerous."

In my view, there is no reason for the typical internet user to directly venture into the Hidden Web—either the Deep Web or the Dark Web within it. But understanding that it exists—particularly in the case of the Dark Web—may help bring home the reality of the threat to your personal information. There is a thriving black market for hacked personal data and full data fingerprints. If yours go missing, now you know where they may end up for sale.

Knowing this will, I hope, motivate you to be more vigilant about your approach to cybersecurity.

NINE

YOUR WEB ACCESS ROUTINE

Digital technology is neither inherently safe nor unsafe, good nor bad. The human factor is critical in balancing the incredible utility of our digital devices and access to the resources of the internet against the potential for personal disruption and harm.

The human in this equation is, of course, you.

In the previous chapters, my objective was to raise your awareness that the door to your personal life may be unlocked—or even wide open. That door is your smartphone, tablet or computer: your gateway to the internet and Web. When we access the internet, it is a two-way connection. The portal to extensive knowledge in the form of Web content is there for the opening, but through that access, we make ourselves somewhat visible and accessible too.

Although most people realize that online access is not in and of itself secure, the results of a survey by Norton found that *one in three users* does not have a password or PIN on their smartphone or computer. About half of those who have taken that single, critical cybersecurity step, then take two steps backward by sharing those access passes with others. The absence, or careless use, of passwords, is the digital equivalent of leaving your keys in the door lock.

Just as surely as if you left the door to your home ajar, when you leave the personal data that is uniquely yours out in the open, you invite complete strangers into your life. Some of them will not have your best interests at heart. Others have been lying in wait for you (meaning *any* potential victim) to make an error in online judgment that they can exploit.

YOUR WEB ACCESS ROUTINE

Symantec suggests that personal internet security " ... is going to be much more [about] 'wellness' ... [and] focused on the routine of prevention rather than looking for a panacea or cure." This is the future: digital well-being and online fitness.

Routine is the key to avoiding much of the pain, embarrassment, and potential harm that can result from online threats. When introducing any new habit into your life, there is a learning curve. The road to mastery of such new challenges can be made much smoother with the creation and following of routines. All you need to do is stay the course until those new approaches become second nature.

If you are saying, "I don't have any routines like that in my life," consider these:

You no doubt have a morning routine. You get up. You grab your smartphone (that is already connected to Wi-Fi or a cellular network) and start your check-in routine. You go to the bathroom. You wash your face. You brush your teeth. You feed the dog. You get a cup of coffee. It's routine.

As a driver, you very likely have a start-the-car routine. You open the door and get in. You put on your seatbelt. You make sure you have your smartphone. If the battery is low, you plug it into the power source. You check the rearview mirror. You start the ignition. You put the car in gear. It's routine.

Your online start-up process can become a standard *Web Access Routine*:

1. Pick up your smartphone and enter your PIN or password, or touch the screen to reveal your fingerprint, to unlock it.
2. Check to see if there are any software, browser or app updates that relate to online safety or security. If they are from known sources, approve their installation. If you are unsure what to do, check with a computer-savvy person you trust.
3. Enter your randomly generated email password (see below), and delete all email from senders you don't know.

4. Enter your separate, also randomly generated, password(s) for your main financial and social media account(s).
5. Dismiss invitations from random wannabe friends or unknown potential connections.
6. Always log off, and log out of your apps and other password-protected accounts.

As you will see in Chapter Ten, there are other actions you can and should integrate into your personal Web Access Routine.

No matter the elements of software, hardware, and apps that help construct a cybersecurity barrier, I remind you of the critical need for trusting your own assessments and judgments. Your ability to make quality decisions based on your unique experiences, learning, and perceptions, must be the foundation for protecting yourself from online harm. This is trusting in yourself—it is *self-reliance*—for the digital age.

Engage your brain and trust your intuition—informed by the facts about personal online cybersecurity. The knowledge base about online threats and how to protect yourself is growing and changing fast. The material in this book is valuable today, but as time goes on it will need to be validated and updated. Now that you have greater awareness, you can be proactive in your own best interest. Choose to be curious about it. Look for the things that can create and improve your personal Web Access Routine.

Once more I remind you of the fighter's admonition: "Protect yourself at all times."

TEN

PERSONAL CYBERSECURITY: WHAT TO DO

*C*YBERCRISIS was written primarily to raise your consciousness about the personal impact of some of the concepts and conditions that may seem far removed from the smartphone in your hand, or from your tablet, computer, or gaming device. However, I would be remiss if I did not offer some "how-to" advice in the form of fundamental cybersafety tips. (As with almost everything in the realm of personal online safety, there are many and varied opinions about what should be part of the routine.)

PERSONAL CYBERSECURITY BASICS

- Use anti-virus and anti-spyware protection for your computers, tablets, smartphone, and even gaming devices.
- Software, operating system, app, and browser security updates are frequent and essential. Download the latest online safety updates and patches when advised by a trusted vendor to do so.
- Load security software that protects kids from clicking on links and sites that could be harmful.
- Configure your home Wi-Fi network to require a unique password for authentication.
- Back up your critical files so that if you are hacked, you may still have access to uninfected versions.
- Monitor your financial accounts, credit card, and credit information, for any unusual activity that could indicate a hack of your personal data.

An excellent resource for personal privacy tips (written in plain English) is offered by TRUSTe, a provider of privacy management solutions. https://www.truste.com/consumer-resources/personal-privacy-tips/. I highly recommend reading it.

PASSWORDS

- Always use passwords and change them often. Put the next date to change your passwords on your calendar. Be sure that everyone in your family, social and work groups do so as well.
- Use complex passwords, including a mix of letters and numbers. A password generator can do this for you. Here is one example, courtesy of Norton: https://identitysafe.norton.com/password-generator#
- Use different passwords for your major online accounts, including banking, health care, government-operated sites and social media.
- Make password management easy on yourself by using a password manager. If you do this, all you have to remember is one password: the one that unlocks the digital vault of your passwords. Here are some ideas: http://www.pcmag.com/article2/0,2817,2407168,00.asp
- For your most important accounts, use two-factor authentication (easier than it sounds). It typically involves receiving a numerical code sent by SMS to your smartphone, to be used along with your password. Here is more information for your consideration. https://www.onionid.com/blog/2-factor-authentication-a-primer/
- Remember to sign out when finished with sites where you must sign in.

EMAIL

- Do not open email messages if you do not recognize the sender. Delete them.

- Never click on links in or attachment to emails, texts, or other internet-borne communications that you do not have a good reason to trust.
- Use a secondary, "spam" email address for enrollment on sites that you believe will want to add you to their email lists (most) and likely send you spam or unwanted advertising.
- Don't send private or sensitive email over public Wi-Fi networks (e.g., the one at your local coffee shop). Also, avoid banking or shopping online from public computers.

SOCIAL NETWORKS

- See the Passwords section above!
- Take advantage of social network privacy-enhancing capabilities and options, and proactively manage them. Under Settings or Options, filter how people can search for you, make comments, see photos tagged with your name, and learn how to block people. Revisit these settings periodically so as to take advantage of the latest options.
- Only accept new invitations you receive on social networks if you know or can qualify the person as trustworthy.
- Minimize your personal information sharing. What you share will become part of your online reputation and precede you in many future situations.
- If you have determined to not be a part of a particular social network any longer, go to the trouble of officially terminating your account and deleting your content.

BROWSER SECURITY AND PRIVACY

Internet browsers have a variety of privacy-enhancing capabilities and options that can be a crucial part of your online protection. Here are links to view the privacy options for some of the major browser providers:

INTERNET EXPLORER / MICROSOFT:
   http://www.microsoft.com/privacy
CHROME / GOOGLE:
   https://www.truste.com/consumer-privacy/personal-privacy-tips/
SAFARI / APPLE:
   http://www.apple.com/safari/features.html# security
FIREFOX / MOZILLA:
   https://support.mozilla.org/en-US/kb/settings-privacy-browsing-history-do-not-track

If you want or need more information, you already know how to get it: Google, Bing and a host of other search engines and websites will take you there. If you want a different, more advanced, or technical approach, simply Google the term "online safety"—about 930,000,000 results will come up. Even just grazing the first few pages of these results, or entering more specific terms, will take you directly to considerably more information than space here permits.

You can download a free copy of this chapter, Personal Cybersecurity: What to Do, from the homepage at www.williamkeiper.com; and you will *not* be asked for or be required to enter any personal data to do so!

GLOSSARY

* * * * *

ADDICTION A state that is characterized by compulsive drug use or compulsive engagement in rewarding behavior, despite negative consequences.

ADWARE A form of spyware that facilitates the display of unwanted advertisements on a screen.

ANTIVIRUS SOFTWARE Software that is used to detect, delete and/or neutralize computer-based viruses.

BOT Software designed to complete a minor but repetitive task automatically or on command.

BOTNET A collection of compromised computers that is built up then unleashed as a distributed denial of service attack or used to send vast quantities of spam.

BYOD Bring your own device: a business policy of allowing employees to connect to a network from personally-owned mobile devices.

CARDING A term describing the trafficking of credit card, bank account, and other personal information online as well as related fraud services. Carding markets have been defined as full-service commercial entities.

CATFISH Someone who creates a fake profile on a social media platform to seduce people.

COMPULSIVE BEHAVIOR Uncontrolled or reactive behavior.

CRACKING Finding a password by running many combinations of characters.

CRISIS A crucial or decisive point or situation; a turning point. An unstable situation, in political, social, economic or military affairs, especially one involving an impending abrupt change.

CYBER Of, or having to do with, the internet.

CYBERBULLYING The use of the internet to harass, intimidate, or cause harm to another.

CYBERCRIME Any crime that is committed using a computer network or hardware device.

CYBERCRISIS (PERSONAL) Any event or series of events relating to or arising from participation in online activities that has led, or could abruptly lead, to a rising level of personal uncertainty and anxiety.

CYBERPSYCHOLOGIST A person concerned with the psychological effects and implications of computer technologies such as the internet and virtual reality.

CYBERSECURITY The processes and methods of protecting a computer or computer network or information by preventing, detecting and responding to attacks.

CYBERSLACKING A term used to describe the utilization of the internet during work hours for unrelated tasks.

CYBERSPACE The internet as a whole.

CYBERSTALKING The use of electronic communications or tracking technologies to stalk or harass another person.

DARK WEB The portion of the Deep Web that is hosted on restricted networks and not accessible using standard Web browsers.

DATA BREACH A data breach is the intentional or unintentional release of secure information to an untrusted environment.

DEEP WEB The part of the World Wide Web that is not indexed by traditional search engines.

DENIAL OF SERVICE ATTACK In computing, a denial-of-service (DoS) attack is an attempt to make a machine or network resource unavailable to its intended users, such as to temporarily or indefinitely interrupt or suspend services of a host connected to the internet.

GIG ECONOMY An economic model in which temporary positions are standard, and organizations contract with independent workers for short-term engagements.

HACK An unauthorized attempt to gain access to an information system.

HACKER An unauthorized user who attempts to or gains access to an information system.

HACKING Use of computers to obtain unauthorized access to data.

HIDDEN WEB The part of the internet that is inaccessible to conventional search engines. Also, known as the *Deep Web*.

IDENTITY THEFT The crime of impersonating someone by using their private information, typically for financial gain.

INTERMITTENT VARIABLE REWARDS Rewards that are handed out inconsistently and occasionally. This usually encourages the person to keep trying or checking until they get what they want, without changing their own behavior.

INTERNET ADDICTIVE BEHAVIOR Compulsive behavior resulting from escalating reliance on internet services or the need to satisfy a craving for internet-related activity. Also called *internet addiction*.

KEYLOGGER A virus, software or hardware that tracks keystrokes and keyboard events to capture private information, passwords or credit card information.

MALWARE Any software used to disrupt computer or mobile operations, gather sensitive information, gain access to private computer systems, or display unwanted advertising

ONLINE DISINHIBITION EFFECT The loosening (or complete abandonment) of social restrictions and inhibitions that would be present in a face-to-face interaction, during interactions with others on the internet.

ONLINE REPUTATION MANAGEMENT Influencing and control of an individual's or business's reputation. Today, primarily an issue related to search results.

PADLOCK Web browsers typically display a locked padlock icon while using the HTTPS protocol (considered more secure than HTTP). While executing secure transactions on the Web, the submitted information is encrypted using public-key cryptography.

PERSONAL CYBERCRISIS Any event or series of events relating to or arising from participation in online activities that has led, or could abruptly lead, to a rising level of personal uncertainty and anxiety.

PHISHING The attempt to acquire sensitive information such as usernames, passwords, and credit card details (and sometimes, indirectly, money), by masquerading as a trustworthy entity in an electronic communication.

ONLINE PREDATOR People who use the internet to hunt for victims to take advantage of them in any way, including sexually, emotionally, psychologically or financially. They seek to manipulate children and others, creating trust and friendship where none should exist.

RANSOMWARE A type of malware that prevents or limits users from accessing their system, either by locking the system's screen or by freezing the user's files unless a ransom is paid.

REAL-LIFE Life outside cyberspace.

REAL-WORLD The physical world, as opposed to the virtual world of the internet.

SCAMMER A person who pursues an online confidence game or other means of deception or fraud, with the objective of a quick payoff for the effort.

SEXTORTION A form of blackmail and sexual exploitation that employs nonphysical forms of coercion by threatening to release sexual images or information to extort sexual favors or money from the victim.

SOCIAL ENGINEERING In the context of information security, psychological manipulation of people into performing actions or divulging confidential information.

SPAM Email that was not requested but was sent to a user and many others, sometimes with malicious intent.

SPAMBOTS Computer program designed to assist in the sending of spam. Spambots usually both create accounts and send spam messages to them.

SPOOFING When an unauthorized person makes an email message appear to be from a known sender by using either the same or a similar address.

SPYWARE Malware that passes information about a computer user's activities to an external device or person.

SURFACE WEB Any part of the World Wide Web that is readily available to the public and searchable with standard internet search engines. Also known as the *Visible or Clear Web*.

TOR (THE ONION ROUTER) Free software designed to make it possible for users to surf the internet anonymously, so their activities and location cannot be discovered by government agencies, corporations, or anyone else.

TROJAN Software that presents itself as an authentic application but carries an item of malware.

TROLL A person deliberately posting malicious or inflammatory messages with the intent to provoke a negative response.

VIRUS A computer program that can replicate itself, infect a computer without permission or knowledge of the user, and then spread or propagate to another computer. A file that is written with the sole intention of doing harm, or for criminal activity.

Definitions in the Glossary were principally sourced from Wikipedia. It is the largest and most popular general reference work on the internet and is ranked among the ten most popular websites. Wikipedia is owned by the nonprofit Wikimedia Foundation.

AUTHOR BIO
WILLIAM KEIPER

William Keiper is an award-winning and bestselling author of creative non-fiction. He is committed to helping individuals and businesses do things differently, as the result of seeing things differently.

He is the author of CYBERCRISIS—*It's Personal Now; Life Expectancy—It's Never Too Late to Change Your Game*; and, *The Power of Urgency—Playing to Win with Proactive Urgency*. He has published a series of short political essays: *Amazon for President, Apple for President*, and *Walmart for President*.

RECOGNITION

WINNER—National Indie Excellence Awards—*Best Personal Growth Book* 2014 (Life Expectancy)

WINNER—The USA Best Book Awards—*Best New Non-Fiction Book* 2012 (Life Expectancy)

WINNER—World Book Awards—*Best Self-Help & Motivational Book* 2012 (Life Expectancy)

WINNER—New York Book Festival—*Best eBook* (all categories, fiction, and non-fiction) 2012 (Life Expectancy)

WINNER—Paris Book Festival—*Best eBook* (all categories, fiction, and non-fiction) 2012 (Life Expectancy)

WINNER—World Book Awards—*Best Business Motivational Book* 2012 (Life Expectancy)

WINNER—World Book Awards—*Best Current Events—Sociopolitical Book* 2012 (Apple for President)

BOOK OF THE YEAR—Living Now Book Awards (Mind) 2012 (Apple for President)

RUNNER-UP—Paris Book Festival—*Best eBook* (all categories fiction, and non-fiction) 2014 (The Power of Urgency)

FINALIST—Next Generation Indie Book Awards—*Best Current Events/Social Change Book* 2012 (Apple for President)

FINALIST—National Indie Excellence Awards—*Best Motivational Business Book* 2014 (The Power of Urgency)

FINALIST—The USA Best Book Awards—*Best Motivational Business Book* 2013 (The Power of Urgency)

FINALIST—London Book Festival—*Best Business Book* 2013 (The Power of Urgency)

FINALIST—National Indie Excellence Awards—*Best Motivational Book* 2014 (The Power of Urgency)

FINALIST—Los Angeles Book Festival—*Best Non-Fiction Book* 2014 (The Power of Urgency)

FINALIST—San Francisco Book Festival—*Best General Non-Fiction Book* 2014 (The Power of Urgency)

FINALIST—The USA Best Book Awards—*Best Current Events Book* 2012, 2013 (Apple for President, Walmart for President)

Made in the USA
Middletown, DE
30 November 2016